NOT UNDER MY WATCH

NOT UNDER MY WATCH

30 Scripture based prayers
to pray over your
children

OLA BEKES

This is my
prayer weapon

© 2023 by Ola Bekes.

All rights reserved. This book or any portion thereof may not be reproduced or used in any manner whatsoever without the express written permission of the author, except for the use of brief quotations in a book review.

Unless otherwise indicated, all Scripture quotations are from the New Living Translation (NLT) bible.

connect with Ola Bekes

olabekes90@gmail.com

Designed & typeset by **Moe**

Instagram: @moeofabuja

Illustrated with assets from

freepik.com

Dedication

First and foremost, I want to thank God Almighty for the sustainability, inspiration, and zeal required to complete this project successfully. Your grace is more than enough for me.

I dedicate this work to Kolawole Bekes, my devoted husband. I appreciate you joining me on this path and sharing this epiphany with me. Beyond what words can express, I love you.

This book is also dedicated to my devoted kids, who gave birth to a new version of me and whom God used to reveal my calling. Royal, Royce, and Royelle. In my heart, you have a special place. And you have my utmost affection.

I dedicate this book to my parents, Mr. Adeyinka and Mrs. Funmilola Balogun, who I will always love. I appreciate you for instructing me in the path of the Lord, giving me clear instructions, and helping me establish a strong foundation. I want you to know that I will always do my best to make you proud.

Acknowledgement

I am grateful to my Apostle, Apostle Joshua Selman, for enlightening me with your teachings and lectures, which have allowed me to bring this book to life.

Thank you for changing the world at large with your incredibly inspirational sermons.

I now have a deeper appreciation and knowledge of God's Word because to you. You're are an excellent teacher.

Contents

A Prayer for Their Health:	1
A Prayer for Longevity of Life:	2
A Prayer for Their inheritance:	3
A Prayer for Greater Grace:	4
A Prayer for Their Mental health:	5
A Prayer for their Purpose:	6
A Prayer for God speed:	8
A prayer For Restoration:	9
A Prayer for Favour:	10
A Prayer for Open doors:	11
A Prayer for their Spiritual lives:	12
A Prayer for their Finance:	13
A Prayer for protection:	14
A Prayer against Fear:	15
A Prayer for Breaking negative repetitive cycles:	16
Prayer against Identity Crises:	17
A Prayer for Mercy:	19

Prayer to be kingdom Financers:	21
A Prayer for Supernatural wisdom:	22
A Prayer to honor:	23
A Prayer for their victory:	25
A Prayer for their Gifts:	25
Prayer for the gift of a Seeing eye:	26
A Prayer for Encounter:	28
A Prayer for Oil:	30
A Prayer to stay in Gods Will:	32
A Prayer for their Heart Desires:	33
A Prayer for a pure heart:	35
A Prayer for Discernment through understanding:	36
A Prayer to be Priests and Kings:	38
A Prayer to remain in the Lord Side:	40

Dear parents,

The book "Not Under My Watch" originated from a point of acknowledging that God had entrusted us with the responsibility of nurturing these children, and that we should watch out for their spiritual, physical, emotional, mental, and intellectual well-being, among other things.

Therefore, I view parenting as a ministry you have been called to so we should not undervalue it ; we are to protect our children by using prayer as a weapon.

In order to help you as parents create a spiritual wall of defence around your kids, this book was put together with you in mind. Because It aims to speak the appropriate words to your children and to help you create the ideal environment in their life.

You have been graced to defend your children in prayers, you have been anointed to fight against the spirits that would desire to steal your children's innocence, and you have the right weapon to wage war against the spirit of Jezebel in the media and in every sphere of life.

YOU ARE A GUARD... and your weapon is prayer. Your children are arrows because you are warriors.

At the gate, they will respond to the adversary

"Children are a gift from the Lord; they are a reward from him. Children born to a young man are like arrows in a warrior's hands. How joyful is the man whose quiver is full of them! He will not be put to shame when he confronts his accusers at the city gates."
Psalms127:3-5NLT

A Prayer for Their Health:

Nevertheless, I will bring health and healing to it; I will heal my people and will let them enjoy abundant peace and security. Jeremiah 33:6

In Jesus name, I declare that my children's bodies are the temples of the Holy Spirit; thus, I command any illness or ailment that is intended to waste my children's lives to leave immediately. Whatever the illness may be or may not be, I command you to go right away in the name of Jesus. I now declare my children are free of cancer, kidney stones, and deadly illnesses of any kind. I declare the blood of Jesus over my children's health, over their body, over their soul, and over their spirit.

Their bodies are not places for sickness or diseases. In the name of Jesus, my children will not experience any kind of mental illness in the present or the future, including anxiety, depression, suicidal thoughts, or self-harm. I proclaim that they have the mark of Christ on their bodies.

They will walk in the purpose you have set for them, they won't be mentally agitated or distressed, and as the grow father, I declare that they have strength and clarity of mind. In the name of Jesus, I decree that they are strong and well, and I pray that the Lord's healing hand will continue to rest upon them. Father, I ask that you maintain them with your grace and might throughout their lives.

A Prayer for Longevity of Life:

With long life I will satisfy him and show him my salvation." Psalm 91:16

Father, I declare that my kids have a covenant of longevity and that their bodies will remain united with their spirits until their time on earth is up. I also curse any early separations brought about by illness, accidents, or the actions of evil people.

I declared that my children would not die young and that they would live to proclaim the works of the Lord in the land of the Living. I pray that the Lord would grant my children a long life and that the enemy has no right to take it away from them. I also declare that my children are wrapped in the lamb's blood, shielded from harm, and that evil eyes are kept at bay.

Father, I declare that my kids will live long, happy lives full of blessings, accomplishments, and a meaningful purpose. I declare that my kids will live happy, fulfilled lives. I declare that I will not cast my young, and that the number of their days that my children will fulfill will be plenty. My children will enjoy long, healthy lives because the death, burial, and resurrection of the Lord Jesus Christ have abolished the power of the dead. Therefore, I decree the cancellation of death over them In Jesus name, Amen.

NOT UNDER MY WATCH

A Prayer for Their inheritance:

O land, land, land, hear the word of the LORD!
Jeremiah 22:29

The portion that God has given to my children is in Jesus' name. I decree that it will gravitate towards their destiny through the ministry of men. I declare that the Lord is my children's inheritance. I decree that lines are falling for them in pleasant places.
I decree that my children have a goodly heritage.

I decree the land will shield its increase for my children, that they will not be cheated in life, they will not be pushed away from their portion, they will enjoy the help of men, wherever they find themselves in the face of the earth they will be favoured because the earth is the Lord's and the fullness thereof, they will inherit their portion, they will eat the good of the land, they will enjoy the fullness of the land.

My children will take pleasure in every bit of land they own, and they won't be without assistance, the Lord will give them people who will ensure their success and assistance. My children will be settled in their place, country, and city by the Lord. In Jesus Name Amen.

A Prayer for Greater Grace:

The grace of the Lord Jesus be with God's people. Amen.
Revelation 22:21

Father, I declare great speed over my children, what others take years will take them days, those around them will see an amplified auction over their lives, their names will not be taken off the good list of life, father manifest in their lives as their lives will be available for you.

They function on the auction of ease and greater grace; grace shall write the story of my children's lives; may God's grace be with them always and sort things out for them. I declare a gracious dispensation over their lives and destiny. Grace will sustain them; it will be their beginning and end. I declare enormous grace over their health, academics, ministry, destiny, family, and career, and grace will fight for them. Grace fights on their behalf, grace protects every organ of their bodies, and finances.

In the name of Jesus, I declare grace over all delays, even in situations where their voices are unheard. Grace is upon their lips, and it will sort my children out. They are finishers because grace completes any good thing they start. In Jesus name. Amen.

A Prayer for Their Mental health:

Do not conform to the pattern of this world but be transformed by the renewing of your mind. Then you will be able to test and approve what God's will is—his good, pleasing and perfect will.
Romans 12:2

I pray for my children's mental health, declaring that as they get older, heaviness of spirit will never be a part of them; the enemy will not steal their joy, the enemy will not bury them in sadness; rivers of living water will continuously flow out of their belly, and joy will continually flow into their lives. As they grow, so will their joy; they will not succumb to the siege of depression; their heart is always full of joy.

In the name of Jesus, I conquer worry, depression, and anxiety and declare that they have a sound mind, their enemies won't attack it, and that they will arise in God's wisdom. I am speaking healing into them on all levels: psychologically, cognitively, spiritually, physically, and socially.

I uproot any sprit of identity crisis and anoint them with a fragrance of gladness and joy. I shut all the wicked portals the enemy tries to exploit to get inside their head. I declare that even as they develop, they won't experience any psychological distress. in Jesus name. Amen.

A Prayer for their Purpose:

I know that you can do all things; no purpose of yours can be thwarted.
Job 42:2

Father, I pray for my children that they will discover their purpose in life at a young age, God will guide them in the right direction, that He will reveal to them the secrets of their life and destiny. He will show them the way, may they receive instructions directly from heaven. He will send my children assistance from Zion as they navigate life, He will always show them the way to the next level. Father, grant them brilliant, inventive, supernatural concepts and strategies that make things work.

They bring those creative thoughts to life by manifesting the fruits of supernatural wisdom and resources. Early on, help them open their eyes and see the way to their future.

Father, set them apart for their mission and show them the path to timely achievement. Let their eyes be opened, their brains be opened to the place of wealth, the secret of the kingdoms, the dimensions of the spirit. Raise help for them about their purpose, give my kids clarity regarding their purpose, and make sure their ears and minds are properly positioned in the spirit that they constantly receive from the throne's impulses. I pray that, by God's mercy, they will be in line with the throne of grace regarding what God has called them to be. What takes others ten years will take them a month, and the grace that will generate wonders in children's lives rests upon them now. The grace for ease and supernatural results rests on them. Father, show my children who they are, where they came from, what they are capable of, and where they are headed. In Jesus name, Amen.

A Prayer for God speed:

He makes my feet like the feet of a deer; he causes me to stand on the heights.
Psalm 18:33

Father, I declare over my children that they will always enjoy a season of speed in their lives, no more delays of any kind as they grow father, allow them access to wisdom and favour. Men will invest their attention in their lives, father arise and have mercy on my children for the time to favour them has come. I dismantle the spirit of procrastination in all its forms, in the form of delays in getting assistance, in business and ministry, in academic pursuits, and in accessing resources. In the name of Jesus, Father, send anyone you need to bring into my children's lives to help and speed them forward; they will not face disgrace or humiliation.

God is sending my children helpers that will enable them to accomplish their goals with speed; God is sending them resources and finances that will enable them to hit their targets and achieve their plans and programs with speed; God is sending them opportunities that will ensure that their life is no longer on the slow lane; they are receiving that blessing that compels and commands speed in a man's life.

Send them a mentor, Father, who will encourage their creativity and introduce them to nations. I pray and eliminate any stumbling obstacles and limits that cause them to sluggishly proceed through life. God of Wonder, help my kids grow and prosper in life. Make them visible. Kings will rise to the brightness of their rising.

A prayer For Restoration:

And the God of all grace, who called you to his eternal glory in Christ, after you have suffered a little while, will himself restore you and make you strong, firm and steadfast. 1 Peter 5:10

In the name of Jesus, Father, I decree and declare by the spirit of grace that my children's lives will be restored; I program a spiritual reality over them and return them to God's original order. Father, all the blessings that are predestined for my children's life appear to them. You connect them to their divine connectors, and they are given the ability to discern who will help them in their destiny. I pray, Lord, that my children are guided to influential men who will put them in the palace, that their voices will be heard there, they have access to talented individuals who will aid in their destiny.

Lord, please provide them the presence of individuals who are willing to support them and bear their load. I pray for my children to be burden bearers for others, divine connectors, influential individuals, and gifted people.

I give my children's life and futures the mantle of grace and speed and rest. In the name of Jesus, everything that wasn't deposited by God in my children's lives should go. They have now been restored. I ask God to give my kids the grace of miraculous healing. I declare that everything that should not have left my children's lives returns through restoration. My children have the grace to pursue, overcome, and reclaim everything. By name of Jesus. Amen.

A Prayer for Favour:

Surely, LORD, you bless the righteous; you surround them with your favor as with a shield.
Psalm 5:12

In the name of Jesus, Father, I decree favour from God's supernatural hand in my children's lives. I command that they never face a drought; instead, they will receive abundant rain, filling their valley to overflowing. My children will not miss their turn, and in the name of Jesus, if they did by the power of God, I take it back to their turn in Jesus' name.

Father, I destroy every negative statement made against my kids because, in Judgement I silent, no weapon created or fashioned against them will succeed, and the devil will not use any negative statement made by a parent, teacher, or anybody else to influence a child's life.

In the name of Jesus, my children will rise above hurtful remarks. They will maintain their spiritual favour and significance; I ask for an unusual favour over my kids' lives. May my female children inherit the mantle of Deborah; may God display his beauty for my children to see. May the blessings of the prophets of old rest upon my offspring. Men who know nothing about my kids will happily provide good news to my kid's helpers. In Jesus name. Amen

A Prayer for Open doors:

Your gates will always stand open, they will never be shut, day or night, so that people may bring you the wealth of the nations their kings led in triumphal procession. Isaiah 60:11

Every door my children encounter will be opened; I open the door of influence for my children, the door of grace for my children, the door of opportunities for my children; for your glory, Lord, open strange doors for my children; Lord, surprise them and intercede for them; may the angel of your presence reach them and perform a miracle. I open every door of barrenness.

I decree every I decree Every force in wicked places to halt results and halt open doors and I challenge it with the blood of the internal covenant. Because my children are the heirs of salvation, I decree and deploy the ministry of angels to every aspect of their life to wage war until triumph is declared, bringing miracles, signs, and wonders.

God will place my children's destiny helpers to love and honour my children, and my children's steps into the realm of prepared benefits. Because open doors indicate access, I order that doors be opened for my children to enter a new season of their life, that all channels to their breakthroughs be flung open, and that I push my children into their testimony.

A Prayer for their Spiritual lives:

The Spirit gives life; the flesh counts for nothing. The words I have spoken to you they are full of the Spirit and life. John 6:63

In the name of Jesus Christ, I pray for grace over their lives of prayer, worship, and the Bible. I pray for supernatural wisdom and understanding. I pray that my children will not be spiritually ignorant and that they will be filled with knowledge of God's view.

I pray that my children reach new heights in their spiritual lives and that there will always be a rising and not a falling. Over My beloved kids, I declare over you the grace to flourish in your spiritual lives. I pray the weight and substance of God's presence rest upon my children, for they will carry God's presence via the power of the Holy Ghost.

In Jesus' name, the grace and the wings of the spirit that will take my children to spiritual dimensions unimaginable, nothing will steal my children's fire, focus, and joy, the gift of the holy ghost work freely in their lives, may they be a wonder to themselves and everyone around them.

A Prayer for their Finance:

But remember the LORD your God, for it is he who gives you the ability to produce wealth, and so confirms his covenant, which he swore to your ancestors, as it is today. Deuteronomy 8:18

In Jesus' name, I command my children's finances to enter strange seasons of wealth and opportunity; in Jesus' name, my children will not fall into any financial pit. I pray that whoever is holding my children's blessings will release them in an unusual way, that everything good that must enter their hands will not elude them, and that they will have boundless breakthrough. Father, I declare that the splendour of my children will be unveiled, as fire from heaven falls on every alter holding the glory of my children. Yesterday will not be better than today for my children.

The outcomes my children will achieve will astound people and draw them to God. I declare the devil to remove his hands from my children's finances, and I declare light over my children's finances, businesses, and careers. I anoint my children's lives with a visibility anointing that will compel others who need them to locate them. I destroy any bad powers preventing my children from obtaining what is meant for them.

Nothing on earth will make the hands of my children empty by the oil of favour, I declare in Jesus' name. I mantle my children's lives with the oil of favour for increase and miraculous provision. Every scattered influence, opportunities, destiny helpers', businesses, and ideas Wherever they are, I command a formation. In Jesus name, I command a financial formation, a spiritual formation, and a destiny formation.

A Prayer for protection:

Whoever dwells in the shelter of the Most High will rest in the shadow of the Almighty. I will say of the LORD, "He is my refuge and my fortress, my God, in whom I trust." Psalm 91:1

In the name of Jesus, Father, I pray for my children's lives. I declare that death will pass over their lives, protecting them from mishaps, kidnapping, plane crashes, and human wickedness. A thousand may fall on their side and ten thousand on their right side I decree only with their eyes will see the reward of the wicked.

I declare that my kids will be strong, totally independent of me and their siblings in adulthood, and I won't feed them when they're old. I also pray for protection over their development, believing that they will grow in stature, intelligence, and understanding.

I pray for protection for my children's reasoning, mental health, friendships, and influence. I also pray that they are not misled. My children are pushed by prophecy, and I push them to realize their destiny and become responsible adults. My children enter a realm of unprecedented grace; the Lord will announce my children; I bestow the "hear ye him" anointing upon them, compelling institutions and systems to come to terms with the acts of God in their lives; and I exponentially increase my children's spiritual influence. My kids won't experience the agony of loss and suffering. Any man who opposes my children spiritually will lose, and my children will triumph over all evils and pitfalls.

A Prayer against Fear:

Be strong and courageous. Do not be afraid or terrified because of them, for the LORD your God goes with you; he will never leave you nor forsake you. Deuteronomy 31:6

In the name of Jesus, I challenge the spirit of fear, and I eternally eliminate fear from my children's lives. I oppose fear of the future, failure, and marriage in my children's lives. I compel all things to work for their good and i come against uncontrollable anger in their life. No force on Earth, I declare will destroy my children's tomorrow. I pray that my children has capacity, endurance, and stamina, as well as the grace to persevere.

Be always their light and salvation. Father, give them stability so they will not flee in the day of battle, give them power and the grace to persist for the sake of their generations. They will have faith in the Lord and in the power of his might.

I crush the works of darkness to always make them fearful, and father help them completely trust you because you will save them from the snare of the fowler, and they will not be terrified of the terror by night or the arrow that flies by day.

A Prayer for Breaking negative repetitive cycles:

"In those days people will no longer say, the parents have eaten sour grapes, and the children's teeth are set on edge.' Jeremiah 31:29

For our struggle is not against flesh and blood, but against the rulers, against the authorities, against the powers of this dark world and against the spiritual forces of evil in the heavenly realms. Ephesians 6:12

In the name of Jesus, I reject in my children's lives cycles of recurring negative patterns that are at odds with God's word. Whether it be illness of any kind, a relapse in a career, or stunted growth, I break these cycles through the anointing of the spirit. I also declare a restoration, declaring that no spirit has any place in my children's lives. In Jesus name, I declare that my children are free from all forms of siege. I also curse the plague of witchcraft and declare that every voice that plots against them has been crucified. Father, I curse every negative pattern of delay, stagnation, failure, limitation, poverty, debt, hardship, and inferiority. I speak Mercy over my kids. I disassociate my kids from negative repetitive patterns because, as I and my kids, we are for signs and wonders, we live for the Lord.

By the God of the heavens, I destroy the operations of poverty and failure at the brink of success. Nothing fails in the hands of my children; they create a new order that will be a transformation. The blood of the everlasting covenant is against the alter of negative cycles. In the name of Jesus, I smash the altars of premature death, procrastination, bareness, and failures in business and career. The glory and destiny of my children. are connected to the throne of grace rather and never connected to the limitations of my bloodline. In Jesus name Amen.

Prayer against Identity Crises:

Do you not know that your bodies are temples of the Holy Spirit, who is in you, whom you have received from God? You are not your own; 20 you were bought at a price. Therefore, honor God with your bodies. 1 Corinthians 6:19-20

Father, show my children who they are in you; let them know that they are the salt of the earth, the epitome of preservation and value, and that they are the light of the world, shining a light for their family, company, generation. My children will not mortgage their destinies to the enemy to be who God has already said they are. My children are the people that God has made them to be.
My children are Co-heirs with God and a joint heir with Christ, far above principalities and powers, they are greatness on the horizon, they are children of God.

I challenge suicidal spirits in my childrens lives as well as the spirits of weariness and discouragement. They will not define themselves based on what they wear, eat, or live in. My children were bought with the blood, and they are miracles in the making. I destroy that spirit that will make my kids desire to modify their sexuality; instead, they will embrace and be proud of their bodies. My children will not stop the order of creation and or wipe away generation because of their choices. I destroy the demon of homosexuality, and it will never lay eyes on any of my children.

I challenge suicidal spirits in my children's lives as well as the spirits of weariness and discouragement. They will not define themselves based on what they wear, eat, or live in. My children were bought with the blood, and they are miracles in the making. I destroy that spirit that will make my kids desire to modify their sexuality; instead, they will embrace and be proud of their bodies. My children will not stop the order of creation and or wipe away generation because of their choices. I destroy the demon of homosexuality, and it will never lay eyes on any of my children. I hide my children in the Almighty's tabernacle. In Jesus name, amen.

A Prayer for Mercy:

The LORD is good to all; he has compassion on all he has made. Psalm 145:9

Father, I pray for mercy for my children, help them realize early in life that they are nothing without you, father by your mercy help my children, thou son of David have mercy on my children and the works of their hands, Let your mercy rest upon their lives so they will lay up gold as dust, my children enjoy mercy in their finances, and spiritual life. Father in their weakness be merciful, redeem their past and present wrong by your mercy, let your mercy authorize your presence in the lives of my Children.

My children will experience God's mercy because their hearts are fixed on him. May he also open doors to growth, healing, expansion, and abundance. May God also reveal to them the treasures of greatness and give them the ability to see and hear.

May God's mercy and blessings be felt throughout their lives. I ask God to hear their prayers and that in their words, they encounter God's mercy and feel greater fire. God's mercy encapsulates their love for God. They only have the desire of the Holy Spirit because the Lord's mercy envelops their desire. My children will not mortgage their destinies to the enemy to be who God has already said they are. My children are the people that God

has made them to be. My children are co-heirs with God and a joint heir with Christ, far above principalities and powers; they are greatness on the horizon, they are children of God in Jesus Name
Amen.

Prayer to be kingdom Financers:

And God is able to bless you abundantly, so that in all things at all times, having all that you need, you will abound in every good work. 2 Corinthians 9:8

I pray and declare that my children will have access to plenty of resources and supplies, they are able to complete tasks, they will always be self-sufficient, and not be financially disabled. With God's grace and assistance, they will have enough money to complete God's work, have the desire and persistence to be kingdom financiers, be seed Sowers in God's house, and be givers rather than takers. I pray that my kids will be empowered in their generation. They won't give in to financial pressure or desperation to the point of compromise.

Lord, grant my children access to sufficiency by the spirit so they can walk in integrity and righteousness all the days of their lives. My children will not be burdened with the Yoke of looking for money, money will look for them, God will bless whatsoever the touch, they are a blessing to others, they are lenders and not borrowers.

God help my children to know how to translate the riches of Christ in glory and to make it manifest in their lives. Lack will not deprive my children from calling the name of the Lord in their generation. my children will not have the lost for money, my children will not lack anything good. My children will finance the gospel, empower them by the spirit to be mighty and robust to the work of the kingdom.

A Prayer for Supernatural wisdom:

Blessed are those who find wisdom, those who gain understanding, for she is more profitable than silver and yields better returns than gold. She is more precious than rubies; nothing you desire can compare with her. Long life is in her right hand; in her left hand are riches and honor.
Her ways are pleasant ways, and all her paths are peace. She is a tree of life to those who take hold of her; those who hold her fast will be blessed. Proverbs 3:13-18

I pray that my children have the wisdom of the spirit, they know how to use prayer to ascend, they will be able to download supernatural wisdom of the spirit directly from heaven, that they will receive and manifest wisdom and power, I decree they will be able to stay in prayers until they receive strategies for the next level, they will be able to hear clearly from God and receive strategies for manifestation, and they will be able to stay in prayers until they receive strategies for manifestation.

I pray that my children will be able to enter the realm of the spirit accurately and readily, and that through the wisdom of God, they will get instructions on what to do directly from God. My children will love the Lord and grow in character to be like Christ; God will give them the insight they need to understand the kingdom and the spiritual life.

A Prayer to honor:

Give him some of your authority so the whole Israelite community will obey him.
Numbers 27:20

I pray for my children that they are full of honour, that they have and understand the principle of honour, that they will not dishonour their parents, pastors, and men of honour, that they carry the anointing that answers to honour, that they will honour their way into realms that will access graces that will put them in charge.

I impact the grace of honour into their lives. I pray that my children will be an effective battle axe and an extension of God's strength, and they have authority over unclean spirits. The grace that quickens the mind, the hand that entices men to make provision for their lives. I bestow that grace onto them. God will raise unusual help to my children and provide them with strategies for advancement. I declare that every disgrace in the lives of my children will be transformed into glory.

A Prayer for their victory:

Finally, be strong in the Lord and in his mighty power. 11 Put on the full armor of God, so that you can take your stand against the devil's schemes. Ephesians 6:10-11

Father, I pray for my children to have the strength to go through seasons and come out victorious, their faith will not falter, they will believe in the Lord with all their hearts, and that they will laugh at every storm. The Lord is their source of strength. Give my children strength and endurance. Give them the grace to weather life's storms; I declare that they are strong in the Lord and in the power of his might.

The grace that raised the rich young ruler will fall on my children and grant them access to the kingdom's keys. In Jesus' name, may the grace to acquire stature and grace, as well as the grace to demand fearful results among the nations, rest upon my children.

I pray in Jesus' name that my children will sort and seek after Jesus, that they will discover Jesus and treasure his presence, that they will not waste the value of his presence, but that it will change their hearts. In Jesus' name, the presence of God will grow within them, causing them to yield to the desire of the Holy Spirit.

A Prayer for their Gifts:

Each of you should use whatever gift you have received to serve others, as faithful stewards of God's grace in its various forms. 1 Peter 4:10

Father in Jesus name, may my children not waste what God has given them, may they believe in their gifts, they are not mare men, but they are gifted with business ideas, they are authors, CEO's, evangelists, that they have a grace carrying mantle, and they will not be useless with the gifts God has given them, they will be true soldiers of Christ.

I declare my children are not empty; they will discover, develop, and utilize their skills to be honoured in life; they are confident and competent in their gifts. My children will have faith in their abilities. They will never engage in harmful rivalry, and they recognize that there is room for them to be who God has called them to be.

My children are gifted, and their gift will make room for them and glorify God. You have given my children the rod of healing, leadership, and creativity, and they will utilize it to your glory. My children's Rod will speak for them in the name of Jesus.

They have the grace to identify, develop, and employ the skills, abilities, gifts, and creativity that God has placed in their spirit. May my children never have or make a reason not to use their gifts. They will use their talents for the glory of God. My children receive grace so that they will not disappoint their generation in business, politics, family, or ministry.

Prayer for the gift of a Seeing eye:

What do you want me to do for you?" Jesus asked him. The blind man said, "Rabbi, I want to see.
Mark 10:51

Lord, open the eyes of children so that they may see, breathe on my children's minds so that their imaginations may come alive, let their creativity and imaginations come alive. I bestow the gift of sight on my children. Father, over my children's faculty of imagination, I declare that something tangible must come out of it that will feed my children's family, something tangible must come out of it that will feed their purposes, creativity arises from the spirit of my children, I declare they are innovative and have ideas for witty inventions. May my children get insight into the intricacies of the written word and discover solutions as they study the Bible. May the Lord open my children's eyes to see in the spirit.

The ability to see prophetically, the ability to see through the eyes of imagination, the ability to take advantage of dreams and visions and rewrite their destiny is upon them in Jesus' name. failure is far from them. Father, give my children an insight of who you have created them to be, bestow in my children a gift of a seeing eyes so they can see their helpers, to choose the right company, to be greater leader. Give my children a seeing eyes, an eye that sees the future, an eye that redeems the future, that has dominion over time.

Open my children's eyes to see which partnership to enter in each given time. teach my children great and mighty things concerning their destinies, future, and families; teach them what they need to be positioned over and what is to come in accordance with each season. The grace to pray in the spirit rests on my children, so that they can begin to download the things that their eyes have not seen, or ears have not heard, so that their dreams and visions are not ordinary, so that their creativity and intelligence advance to another level, so that the capacity to draw insight from the word is enhanced.

Open my children's eyes to understand where the difficulties are, where their spouse is, and their ideas associated with their money. By the gift of sight may my children not fall in danger, the enemy shall not take advantage of my children's seeing eye.

A Prayer for Encounter:

I keep asking that the God of our Lord Jesus Christ, the glorious Father, may give you the Spirit of wisdom and revelation, so that you may know him better. 18 I pray that the eyes of your heart may be enlightened in order that you may know the hope to which he has called you, the riches of his glorious inheritance in his holy people, 19 and his incomparably great power for us who believe.
That power is the same as the mighty strength.
Ephesians 1:17-19

Father, in the name of Jesus, I declare that my children will have an encounter with a great dimension of God, and that the direction of their exploits will be great. Father, reveal yourself to my children, reveal your favour, blessing, power, and their prophetic blueprints in you. Allow your light from your word to meet them and guide them to what was written about their destiny in your word.

Father, give my children wisdom and revelation from your knowledge as they develop; may the eyes of my children's intellect be enlightened; and may my children comprehend the hope of their calling and the riches of their inheritance as saints. Baptize my children with the spirit of revelations, and my children will have eyes to see beyond the letters and verses as they study the word.

As a parent, I proclaim that I will not give birth to armed robbers, and that my womb will not produce evildoers and devils. In the name of Jesus only kings emerge from my loins. Every weird thing not planted by God in my children's lives, businesses, and ministries is declared to be removed. May God stop anyone who will communicate incorrect things to the destiny helper of my children.

A Prayer for Oil:

And take some blood from the altar and some of the anointing oil and sprinkle it on Aaron and his garments and on his sons and their garments. Then he and his sons and their garments will be consecrated. Exodus 29:21

father I declare over my children's destiny that they receive new oil over their destiny; give my children oil for their gifts, ideas, ministries, businesses, and callings; and give my children oil to continue praying and learning. new oil is on their head and lamp so they can continue to burn for you. Lord, anoint them to persevere in the face of adversity.

My children's sleep will be refreshing, they will have encounters with the spirit of God, revelations and secrets will be revealed to them, they will wake up rejuvenated and with plans for the next ten years of their life, business, and destiny. Give my children a sleep of impartation, reprogram my children in their sleep, and they will be all ways prophetic, encountering divine direction, as Daniel did.

God will communicate to them as they sleep. Anoint their hands so that their exploits will bring glory to God and glorify Jesus. Father, do something tangible through the lives of my children that will draw Men to Jesus, grant access to the supernatural workings of the spirit in their lives, and empower them for kingdom exploits. The impact of my children will be loud enough to draw many to Christ, as gentiles are coming to see their light and monarchs are rising to prominence.

A Prayer to stay in Gods Will:

For I know the plans I have for you," declares the LORD, "plans to prosper you and not to harm you, plans to give you hope and a future.

Jeremiah 29:11

Father, in the name of Jesus, reveal your will to my children in clarity, Father, direct them, give them precision of understanding of your will, they will rely on your will so that the grace for lifting and enthronement rest upon them, manifest your will on their life so that they do not fight unnecessary battles.

Father, they will continue to love you even in their season of waiting; help them to be firm in you regardless of their season; let my children understand that their compensation is in their waiting; grant them the grace to be patient.

Help my children understand that they are working in purpose regardless of the season. Help my children to be grateful in all circumstances because you are preparing a table for them and fixing things on their behalf.

As a trophy, reveal my children in due time. Father, help my children fight unseen battles and avert certain dangers the enemy has programmed ahead of my children as they follow in your will. Help, my children to stay in your will.

A Prayer for their Heart Desires:

For where your treasure is, there your heart will be also.
Matthew 6:21

Where your heart is, there is your treasures. Father, as my children grow, may they yield to the direction of the Holy Spirit rather than the pressures of their generation, and may their hearts be passionately in love with Jesus. May they desire to see God glorified more than desire for fame, success, achievement, or a noble testimony.

May these not be their fundamental desires; instead, may my children constantly wish to bring blessing and significance to others. May my children's desires be motivated by their love for Jesus rather than by a desire to be famous and successful; they will love God above all else. Their lives will be like an oasis in the desert. Father, vet and purify my children's hearts; attachment to money, reputation, and ordinary things will be far from them; worldly things will not capture their hearts and desire.

Circumcise their heart and purify their intentions from a young age by separating their heart from fame, worldly money, and aspirations for increases against their love for God. They will be far from spiritual activities, and their passion will be edited so that Jesus will be the epic centre, and Jesus will be the reason for prayer, fasting, ministry, and influence. They are centred on Jesus' love. In Jesus' name, I decree and declare that the voice of God will be a primary source of motivation. They will not bow to the pressures of their generation, but instead take up the cross and follow Jesus as their shepherd.

A Prayer for a pure heart:

Blessed are the pure in heart, for they will see God.
Mathew 5:8

Lord Touch my children's hearts, may their intentions be pure, so they can see you. Lord come through for them, may they see you lift, so they can realize there is no limit to what God can do. Lord, come as a refiner fire andt purify their hearts. Father, purge my children's hearts and intentions so that their lives will be a project to reveal you rather than their flesh and ego. May their life reflect Jesus.

Use my children as a battle axe to alter their generation because they have been refined; use my children as saviours for their families and generation because they have submitted to you; and use my children as saviours for their families and generation because they have submitted to you. I proclaim my children are light, and they shine even in the dark, because of the concentration of their hearts. The anointing that speaks rest upon my children

A Prayer for Discernment through understanding:

And this is my prayer: that your love may abound more and more in knowledge and depth of insight, 10 so that you may be able to discern what is best and may be pure and blameless until the day of Christ.

Philippians 1:9-10

Father, in Jesus' name, may my children be able to maximize their seasons, may they not be devoid of discernment, and may they possess the faculty of spiritual insight. I declare that their organs have been educated to detect spiritual impulses; may they have the ability to know what God is doing as well as what the enemy is doing.

In the name of Jesus, may the grace to discern instructions for their destiny rest on my children; may my children never go where God is not because of a lack of discernment; and may my children get the tactics for every season and their dominion. Father, open my children's eyes to see the formula of their dominion this season, that they get by the spirit strategies to succeed in ministry, business, and raising their families, the strategies that control blessings every season are upon them.

My children's ability to receive instructions on what to do at all times helps them recognize signals and techniques that give them power.
I pray that my children has the ability to have the insight to know when to watch and

when to pray, that they will be slow to speak and quick to listen, so that their words have life and power. May my children not have a victim mindset, may the mantle of Daniel rest on my children, and may their significance not be diminished.

A Prayer to be Priests and Kings:

You have made them to be a kingdom and priests to serve our God, and they will reign on the earth."
Revelation 5:10

But you are a chosen people, a royal priesthood, a holy nation, God's special possession, that you may declare the praises of him who called you out of darkness into his wonderful light. 1 Peter 2:9

In the name of Jesus, Father, I give my kids the discipline to freely offer themselves in prayer and the word, to freely engage in spiritual fellowship, and let it rest upon them as priests. My children have the same genuine wisdom as priests; therefore they are able to access secrets that are kept in hidden places. I declare that they are prepared to make the sacrifices that priests carry out.

May my children be endowed with power from on high that puts them in command of situations and circumstances in Jesus' name, that they are able to compel things to be consistent with God's will, that they have the power to subdue every force of darkness that wants to oppose their purposes on earth, and that they are empowered by God's spirits. My children enjoy favour that unlocks unusual doors, commands access and acceptance, and grants them uncommon kindness. They gain favour and are preferred above all others. My children have the grace of honour, the one who compels royalty.

May their priesthood empower their kingdom, May the lord touch their crown and the sceptre., they are priests, kings, and prophets. Father, decorate my children for the throne. My children are the royal priesthoods and a chosen generation.

A Prayer to remain in the Lord Side:

So, he stood at the entrance to the camp and said, "Whoever is for the LORD, come to me." And all the Levites rallied to him. Exodus 32;26

Yet to all who did receive him, to those who believed in his name, he gave the right to become children of God—children born not of natural descent, nor of human decision or a husband's will, but born of God. John 1:12

Father, in the name of Jesus, I declare that my children will remain on the Lord's side all the days of their lives, just as Gideon became a warrior, Joseph became a king, Daniel became one of the presidents, and Esther reigned as queens by obtaining favour from the Lord. Lord, no matter what occurs, my children will remain on the Lord's side, because the Lord's side brings rest all around, they stand in integrity, my children will pick the Lord's side, they do ministry, business, and increase in wealth while standing on the Lord's side.

Because they are on the Lord's side, they enjoy protection, triumph, joy, delights, peace, and power over their foes. I declare that because they are on the Lord's side and have a functional connection with Jesus, my children will receive the gift of forgiveness and eternal life through Jesus. Because they are on the Lord's side, they will encounter Salvation, they will have a desire to win others to the Lord's side, and they will have access to the life of God (ZOE) because they are on the Lord's side. Because they are on God's side, the power of addiction is far from them; they are truly free because they are on God's side.

My Prayer Requests

Hevavenly Father _____

_____

_____

_____

_____

_____

_____

_____

_____

_____

_____

_____

My Prayer Requests

Hevavenly Father ⸺

My Prayer Requests

Hevavenly Father ⸺

My Prayer Requests

Hevavenly Father ───────────────

_____

_____

_____

_____

_____

_____

_____

_____

_____

_____

_____

www.ingramcontent.com/pod-product-compliance
Lightning Source LLC
Chambersburg PA
CBHW041812040426
42450CB00001B/4